THE BURNING MOUSTACHE

The Burning Moustache

A collection of poems
by
PHILIP WEXLER

Adelaide Books
New York / Lisbon
2020

THE BURNING MOUSTACHE
A collection of poems
By Philip Wexler

Copyright © by Philip Wexler
Cover design © 2020 Adelaide Books

Published by Adelaide Books, New York / Lisbon
adelaidebooks.org

Editor-in-Chief
Stevan V. Nikolic

All rights reserved. No part of this book may be reproduced in any manner whatsoever without written permission from the author except in the case of brief quotations embodied in critical articles and reviews.

For any information, please address Adelaide Books
at info@adelaidebooks.org
or write to:
Adelaide Books
244 Fifth Ave. Suite D27
New York, NY, 10001

ISBN: 978-1-952570-55-1

Printed in the United States of America

For Nancy, Jake, Mom, Will and Gigi

And a Further Dedication

To the many direct and indirect casualties of the 2020 COVID-19 global pandemic and the brave, caring, and generous individuals sacrificing their own well-being to help us get through it and return to a semblance of normalcy.

Giving Way

Villanelle for a Global Pandemic, 2020

The roots that grounded us together shift.
Like islands we're advised to keep apart.
There is no telling how far we may drift,

How long until our breath strained spirits lift
And we come back to dancing heart to heart?
The roots that grounded us together shift.

Too suddenly did fault turn into rift.
Where is the ending to this endless start?
And who can tell how long we'll be adrift?

When will, afresh, a touch become a gift?
The final course is not for us to chart.
The roots that grounded us together shift.

From near to far, the switch was lightning swift.
A germ, no more, upset the apple cart.
There is no telling how far it may drift.

We don our masks and practice daily thrift,
Keep our distance, play our given part.
The roots that grounded us together shift.
Still, back together we must surely drift.

Contents

Giving Way   7

Credits   13

I

The Phoenix   *17*

Night of Down (Berlin - November 9, 1938)   *19*

Enduring Collapse   *22*

The Last Hopes of Greco Pirelli   *25*

Marshmallows and Red Wine   *27*

Legacy of the Great Man   *29*

Brief Departure   *31*

Sailing   *33*

Consequences   *35*

I Hear Choppers   *37*

Marked Down   *39*

Gulp (or Chinese Restaurant Encounter)   *40*

Glimpses of Brooklyn *42*

Drunken Japanese Warrior Fantasy *43*

Cleaning Lobby Windows *45*

Lantern Festival in Rain *46*

Yellow Comfort *48*

The Leash *50*

Final Closing Sale, Really, Final *51*

Change of Address *53*

A Perfect Pair *55*

II

Winter *61*

Outliers *63*

Focus *65*

November Brown *66*

Prayer for the Windlorn *67*

The Bay *69*

Modigliani is Bread *70*

The Man with the Burning Moustache *71*

Complexities *72*

Make Believe *74*

Aquatic Airs *76*

Before Clearing Snow *78*

III

A Closer Look   *83*

Museum Going   *85*

Snow on Fifth Avenue   *86*

Under a Flowering Pear Tree at a Stubborn Red Light   *89*

What the Zoo Holds   *91*

grandmother in sweater   *92*

Fishing by Mistake   *93*

The Calling   *95*

The Kitten   *98*

Grandmother with Tubes   *100*

Stray Bullet   *102*

Swamp Monster   *104*

Tousle-Haired Kid   *106*

The Little Princess was Running   *108*

IV

The Ball Rolling   *113*

Bounty   *114*

Archaeology   *116*

Midnight Watch   *117*

The Pears   *118*

Silk   *119*

Snow *121*

star magnolia *122*

Gelato *123*

Combing *125*

Already There *127*

Cashmere *129*

Broken Yellow *131*

Inside the Picket Fence *133*

Autumn Knowledge *134*

Eating Kisses *135*

Their Morning in Flannels *137*

Out Back *139*

The Continuity of Disentanglement *140*

Chives *142*

Perfectly Blind *144*

The Connection *145*

Turn Out the Light *147*

About the Author *149*

Credits

Some of these poems or earlier versions thereof
have been published in:

Big Windows, Other Voices, Edgz, Parting
Gifts, Poetry Salzburg Review,
Sand, Karamu, Third Wednesday, Mobius,
Great American Poetry Show, Great American Poetry Show 2,
Qutub Minar, Adelaide Magazine,
Heart Lodge, Chiron Review, Amulet, Tar River Poetry,
Snail Mail Review, Timber Creek Review, Rockhurst Review,
ProCreation, Off the Coast, Loch Haven Review, Ellipsis,
Autumn Harvest, Common Ground
Review, Homestead Review,
Ice Cream Poems (anthology), Indigo
Rising, Rent-a-Chicken Speaks,
Oasis, I-70 Review, Mad Poets Review, Sheila-Na-Gig,
Connecticut River Review, Axe Factory Review

I

The Phoenix

Bit by heavenly bit, I overcome
the rules of flight and gravity,

of life and death. I plunge
from dizzying heights alone,

dependent on my memories, off-
kilter, without context to the flames,

but sure I've seen destruction
once before, or many times.

I don't decide to ground myself
in splinters, charred, detached

from my secure surrounding skin
but why resist? Nor do I expect

to stay aloft, forever intact,
persistent, never looking back.

From an egg of uncertainty,
spinning this way and that,

doubt hatches but its course
and end are not foretold. I shake

Philip Wexler

and roll the dice but guess
in vain, and inklings prove false

yet again. Embers don't disclose
what they enfold. I dare not

fault what's meant to be but
can't endure through ages

on a whim. I find myself back
in a place I've lost and found

a thousand times before,
am ashen from the fear I will

be too used up by hopeless
wandering to ever close

a deal. And then, deluded
once more as I soar, I fall

for a vision, shining and bright,
a flash, no more. The phoenix

does not choose to be
consumed and dreads

each death as if
there were no rising.

Night of Down (Berlin - November 9, 1938)

The feathers, the down, more
than anything else, I remember.

Historians these days they talk only
about shattered glass, official havoc,

sanctioned confusion,
an incessant din. Yes, maybe

we heard some breaking, shouting,
faintly from the main streets.

But the neighbors who dropped by
without knocking, using, we were sure,

a master key from the none too friendly
landlord, spoke little, broke no glass.

The clatter they made pulling out
drawers and overturning tables was faint.

Softer still were the sounds of the quilts,
blankets, and pillows they ripped.

This part they undertook with gusto.
They were like children, shaking fluff

Philip Wexler

from room to room, down hallways
and stairs, out the windows

of our apartment to blanket
the streets, a softly falling snow.

In my life, I never paid any mind
to the insides of our bedding,

but that night, after we gave up
pleading with them to stop,

we stood aside, spectators,
and I mourned

the slaughter of all the geese
I ever ate. This scattered plumage,

their coats in life, was the filling
we slept on and underneath as,

on other occasions we stuffed
their bare-skinned bodies destined

for roasting with chestnuts and prunes,
all for our ultimate consumption,

which I now can't help but regret.
Poor fowl, sustaining us with their lives,

their downfall and ours. The neighbors
shook hands for a job rightly done, and left,

returning to their reign of indifference.
No storm troopers these; just simple folk.

Once the flurries subsided, my husband
pressed his forehead against the upper pane

of the cold kitchen window, his eyes shut.
Our son, I released from the foyer closet.

He ran about, joyfully tossing as good as
weightless white clusters over his head,

exclaiming that it was a blizzard
and racing out to lasso in his friends.

I sat on the floor in a drift,
feeling what it's like to be plucked

when there are no more
feathers to give.

Enduring Collapse

(9/11/2001 – Towers within sight of Pool Hall)

Just as old Charley neatly drops
the eight ball in a side pocket,
I hear the world fracture outside

and in, and the mostly ignored TV
in the corner cuts to breaking news.
We abandon the shabby felt table,

heave up the grime smeared window,
and shove yesterday's crushed soda
cans, crookedly lined up on the sill,

to the floor. Joined by the other
hustlers, we watch in the distance
the event mirrored on TV

unfold in real space. We shift
our view back and forth,
listening to commentators

on the air no less dumbfounded
than us. I feel the second impact
in my solar plexus, am short

THE BURNING MOUSTACHE

of breath at the tumbling down
and the dark unforgiveable
plumes ascending. On the screen

the conflagration is replayed,
replayed, replayed. I choke
on the distant view of billowing

smoke and wade through ashen
numbness. We huddle in front
of the window like billiard balls

in a rack, grip cues, chalk, anything
as amulets to keep us from vaporizing.
In the sound of far-off sirens

I hear the looming question, "Why?"
but it's too soon to dig motive
out of the debris. Unnerved,

I can't stop watching. After a time,
we recover our personal spaces,
disperse, make calls, exit one by one.

Soon it's only old Charley and me,
transfixed. All I can believe in
is my disbelief. Amid the commotion,

there is stillness here as balls no longer
clack against balls. Their colors,
solid, striped, littering green fields,

coalesce to gray, a lingering
afterimage. Damage is yet to be
tabulated, names named, victims,

perpetrators, and tolls taken.
But old Charley has had
enough, says now he's seen it all,

puts his green poker visor back on,
returns to our table, racks up
the balls anew, takes his break shot.

I turn his way at the sound, see numbers
swirling, dark matter, event horizons,
black holes, balls hovering on edges,

drifting clouds of smoke, and work
at keeping my balance. He steps back,
surveys the configuration. I realize

he is waiting for me and asks, finally,
if I'm in or out. I chalk up the tip
of my cue. The blue never looked

as intense. My ears are fully attuned
to the TV but my eyes are on the table.
"Two ball, corner pocket," I answer, and shoot.

The Last Hopes of Greco Pirelli

Were that summer would not be
like winter as it had been
that summer and that winter
would be more like summer
as it rarely was,

that the train from Bergamo
to Milan would leave on time
just once and that the stars
would be free from cloud cover
on the nights we need them most

and blanketed when their bright
beauty caused too much pain,
that Mrs. Pirelli would pay
more attention to the cat -
it strays so often,

and, of course, that Sunday
would not be so equivocal a day,
pulling this way and that.
These were the last hopes
he told to no one.

On a cool August Sunday morning,
Mr. Pirelli left town

Philip Wexler

in a fine wooden coach driven
parallel to the quiet railroad tracks.
Mrs. Pirelli sat next to the driver.

She had forgotten to feed the cat.
As it grew dark the stars sparkled
in a sky clear as the lake reflecting them.
The road was bumpy and hard to follow
but Mr. Pirelli knew it with his eyes closed.

Marshmallows and Red Wine

With balalaika music, my companions
and I, we pass our routine Sunday night

at the bistro, with Chianti, marshmallows,
and fevered talk of what is impending.

I notice the grenade rolling across
the floor to the other side of the table,

but nothing sensible registers, until
all at once, there they lay, my friends,

sleeping with marshmallows,
communing with angels, the table

itself intact, the bottle of wine still
upright, and the rose with the truncated

stem as centered in the teacup
as before but more fragrant.

I swallow the marshmallow
I was chewing. Who could fault me

for that? It's mostly air, like so much
else I've bounced up against these days.

Philip Wexler

I gulp some wine before bending
over the bodies. Everyone else

is long gone. A voice at the window
shouts to me to get the hell away.

I hear a faint siren, and sit back down,
pour myself more wine, and sip

as the ghosts of the dead, incredulous,
watch my every move.

Legacy of the Great Man

The mansion where the great man slept,
entertained, was untidy, scrutinized
esoteric books and stockpiled
his vast fortune accumulated by years
of backstabbing and deeds of no good,
is administered by a trust fund
that admits for scholarly research
only those visitors willing to spend
a month in the mansion, eating what
the great man ate, sleeping where he slept,
reading his books, contributing commentary
to the guest book and cash to the estate.
Moreover, they must pledge to go out
into that great world in the guise
of the great man himself, outfitted
with his papers, forging new identities,
undergoing surgical reconstructions,
each a replica of the great man,
down to the scars on his groin,
and wherever they are sent they must
conduct themselves as reprehensibly
as he did, destroy hearts, families,
and corporations, as he relished doing,
and crumble empires, as he aspired to.
When they finally expire, for good
that is, their bodies must be preserved

Philip Wexler

by the resident taxidermy clinic
which will stiffen them nicely
and create plausibly licentious poses
to approximate the great man
as he must have looked just before
his own body vanished from sight
as, it was variously rumored,
in a boating accident on the high seas,
a plane wreck over a polar ice cap,
or the pit of an active Hawaiian volcano,
where some claimed it turned to ash
and fertilized the pineapple plantations
he bought and sold with abandon.

Brief Departure

You are called away from the table.
It must be the long-awaited telegram

that would alter your life. The dinner
conversation about the housing market

doesn't skip a beat as you hurry off.
Your fork with its last flaky chunk

of salmon hovers in mid-air. Chardonnay
keeps flowing from the bottle the actress

holds over your crystal goblet, never
filling up. The tapered candles cast

a flickering rosy glow on expressionless
faces, and forfeit no wax in your absence.

You fairly gallop down the spiral staircase,
thrilled to be summoned for the news at last.

The table, after all, was tiresome, a stop-
gap measure at best. Your mind wasn't on it,

the chatter, the nonsense. You have no regrets
about leaving. Already you see a cornucopia

Philip Wexler

of possibilities - purpose, depth, relevance–
as you prepare to exchange the frivolous

for meaning. You feel yourself grabbing
hold even in the antechamber but the door

closes as you are steps away, the butler
offering his regrets. It was all a mistake.

The telegram was for the villa next door.
Resigned, you go back, no one the wiser,

take up where you left off, finish the salmon,
sip the wine, complain that your chateau

outside Paris hasn't sold for months.
The faces resume their chewing, nod

in empathy and grow less rosy as candles
melt down to their bitter ends.

Sailing

Who on the shaky boat,
would have cared to dance
with me anyway, with the night

so late, strangers already
in each other's arms,
and the smashed musicians

improvising sloppily
in between trips to the bar.
So, struggling to keep balance

myself, *bottoms up*, I toast
with the last of my scotch.
I take to the deck and revive

in the growling wind. Out
in the open, the captain's
infant daughter, on all fours,

slides along the slippery,
pitching surface, unable
to snatch the pacifier

she let drop. Her mother,
oblivious, grabs a handrail
and contemplates the deep,

Philip Wexler

rocking and tilting in time
to the pipe-smoking captain
snug in his quarters,

the cocktail waitress calling
from his anteroom
that she won't be but a moment.

I am absorbed by the choppiness
of the waves, the mournful
foghorn and Mycenaean sailors

carousing at the edges
of their known world,
and by Cleopatra, still a slip

of a girl on an Egyptian
galley amusing herself
with a cageful of asps.

It's refreshing to sail
through the night sky
where past and future stars

intertwine. The water's antics
are benign, and it's bracing
to have it splash on my face.

What jolts me more
than any squall is grasping
that there is anything at all.

Consequences

The man yanked the dog
whenever it made a misstep
as if the weight of the world

were upon him. The animal
was obedient as dogs go but
a ripe aroma might make it

veer from the dictated route.
An unsanctioned sniff here,
there, and the man would jerk

the chain out of proportion
to the misdeed, torquing
the dog's neck sharply.

He did not say a word, though one
could sense he swallowed volumes
of grievances, and more

was waiting for the dog at home.
One could see it in his shoulders,
hunched, tense, and his grimace,

and tell that he was storing
up every insult and injury
he'd ever suffered, and that

Philip Wexler

the dog, growing weaker, thinner
by the day, was his vent.
After a time, it gave up on smells,

looked ahead blankly
or quizzically up at the man,
wondering what came next.

One day the man walked dogless,
the same route, a fist clenched as if
gripping something or ready to strike.

I Hear Choppers

Sirens, these days more
than ever, rampages, snipers,
prisons emptied, inmates
on the loose, low flyers
overhead, surveillance even
when I bury myself
in blankets, duck left, right,
crouch, dive into water. Still
I'm tracked by radar. Subs
tail me, and in the gurgling
depths the muted sounds
of choppers. I pop up sopping
to check if they've gone. Fat
chance. Relentlessly, they cut
swaths of sky. I'm buffeted
by boulders of air. The pressure
strains my ears, makes my blood
bubble. Police, helmeted,
shielded, reckless, wild, clatter
in the streets. The masked army
of desperados pick off the weak,
slow, feeble. Amphibious vehicles
smash each other like bumper cars.
I sidestep landmines, and bullets
graze my genitals. The atmosphere
reeks of thermonuclear threat

Philip Wexler

and an aura of apocalypse
is pervasive. Scopes track me
every which way. Every living,
dead, body, a target. Triggers
poised, pumped. Cross-hairs
positioned. Sleeping, waking,
doesn't matter. Enemies, friends.
No telling one from the other.

Marked Down

The elegantly tailored young hostess,
in golden evening dress, red silk
around her shoulders, smiling, cool,
not a thread out of place, welcoming
everyone with perfect manners and charm,
more a princess than the real article,
moving with ease and grace, inspiring
the ladies' admiration, not envy,
making gentlemen of boors, gladly
receiving kisses on her hand, and flattery
with modesty and good humor, a study
in sophistication and style, no bead of sweat
marring her brow, no hair out of place,
an immaculate vision of loveliness,
tending to her guests, never resting
until, for a breath of fresh garden air,
she fairly glides toward the louver doors,
slips off the silk from her shoulders
and drapes it lightly on the outstretched
arm of the marble statue of Aphrodite,
and as she passes, everyone stares
at the stiff white label sticking up
from the back neckline of her dress,
with the name "Lorenzo" inverted,
and next to it a red dot as if
it had been marked down.

Gulp (or Chinese Restaurant Encounter)

Suddenly a cockroach big
as a fortune cookie was crawling
across the table headed
for my egg rolls so I gulped
down the barbecued pork
I was chewing, grabbed
a sharp chopstick and thrust
it straight down the intruder's
back. Alive, it scuttled
away from my meal
with the stick protruding
from its back like a flagpole
without a flag. At the edge
of the table, it paused,
dropped to the floor
right side up and continued
in a kind of drunken stagger
through the restaurant
and out the door, politely
held open by a waiter,
as if this were a daily occurrence.
Miraculously, the roach
was not trampled by the coming
and going feet. I watched
it continue to the curb
and begin to cross the street.

THE BURNING MOUSTACHE

At that distance and
with the traffic, I couldn't see
it well anymore. Feeling a bit guilty,
I decided to interrupt
my second course
of roast duck to locate the bug.
There might be time to hurry it
to a roach rescue group.
But I couldn't find a trace
of the massive black body,
neither squashed nor intact,
only a nicked and slimy chopstick
across the street, in front
of the newsstand, where
on its awning a crow was looking
down at me, and …
crowing.

Glimpses of Brooklyn

1.

In the Dumbo liquor store, the salesman
touted the new Korbel XS blended brandy's
sweet smoothness and appeal to the ladies.
But what sold me was hearing that it wasn't
even available in the Bronx yet. Talk about
being ahead of the curve!

2.

At the newsstand in Gravesend, I pulled
a Sunday New York Times from the middle
of the pile and asked the shady looking proprietor,
my friend, for three Mega Millions lottery tickets.
"To stay or to go?" he asked. I smiled. He caught
my drift and slipped me a small plastic bag.

3.

At the outdoor cafe in Park Slope, two old men.
One complained incessantly about his wife.
The other didn't say a word in reply. "So, how
are your ears doing, Hank?" the first asked
the other. "Damn," he said, watching a woman
loading her car trunk, "what a behind!"

Drunken Japanese Warrior Fantasy

Roasted octopus brain over seaweed,
served up cold with rice, and a little
blue and white porcelain bottle
of sake refilled you forget how
many times, and you smack your hand
down on the ancient wood planks
carved with a hundred hatch marks
of your sword, one for each vanquished
foe, and think, "Good thing they were
stopped in their tracks," and you take
another bite of brain, seaweed hanging
from the corner of your mouth, and
call the wench of a hostess who used
to be a refined geisha until you broke
her in, and give her a fond but
no nonsense slap on the behind, telling
her no, you don't need another thing,
it's getting late after all and there
are still battles to fight and enemies
to subdue, so you stagger out,
sword drawn, slicing the air, alert
in your besotted way for suspicious
strangers, but all is still this night
with light snow just starting to fall
as you reach the door of the old
barn where you'll bed down

Philip Wexler

for the night, except you don't
even realize about the snow, think
the moisture on your beard is sake,
not melting flakes, and smell
quite literally a plot being hatched
by a rival gang before it hits you
that it's the aroma of the octopus
brain you are regurgitating,
but you keep your eyes glued
to the hay piles, just daring anyone
to emerge from hiding, and you lean,
a little off balance but primed
for battle, not to be underestimated,
and ready, at the least, to take on sleep.

Cleaning Lobby Windows

Their morning job starts on either side
of massive office building panes
of clear, thick glass. Inside, looking
out, he sprays a rag and wipes
in overlapping circles. Eager for fresh
air, she takes her station outside, looking
in, no matter the wind chilling her back
and snow blowing into the colonnade.
She is slight, delicate but single-minded.
She sprays the glass and traces crisscross
patterns with a sponge. They avoid looking
at each other. Even with a stepstool,
she must stretch to reach the very top.
She feels a shoulder muscle snap, and yelps.
He doesn't hear. She steps down and sits
on the stool, turning her back to the window.
She watches the snow, feels it drift around
her ankles, and puff onto her face. Now
he looks at her, traces with his cloth
on the glass, the motion of her hand massaging
her shoulder, and sees her hair and neck, as if
for the first time. She dreams of a better job
where she could conserve her energy.
He wonders if he could support the both of them.
He knocks on the glass and motions her in.

Lantern Festival in Rain

Monkeys, turtles, cranes of silk and paper artificially
glowing from within, splash color on an afternoon
bereft of much, counterpoint to the Chinese garden's
damp and muted natural shades, its gray-brown
pebbled paths and shrubs of few toned greens.

Outside the Pale Mountain Pavilion, an old man
in two trench coats, one draped over another, sells
jasmine tea and rice dumplings to take off the chill.
I tuck a wet umbrella under my arm and fumble
for cash. Refills, he says, though not of what, are free.

In the Pavilion, a slender girl bends over a gu-zheng,
red and black lacquered. The string instrument sits
on a saw-horse frame next to a stack of her recordings.
She sings in an exotic wavering style. Potted
chrysanthemums and dragonfly kites hang from rafters.

What tea is left I take out in the recalcitrant rain.
At the pond, back under my umbrella, I sip
and view the giant floating dragon, green and fire
breathing, bedecked in layered necklaces of pin-prick
lights. I crumple the empty paper cup, stuff it

in my pocket. I lean against a taut, thick rope
of hemp beside the water's edge and watch white koi

rise to the surface. Next to me, gripping her own umbrella in two fists, the gu-zheng musician, on break, studies the misty sky. Her recorded songs are piped

through speakers on the ground. At a puff of wind, barrel lanterns of yellow and blue on the far side of the pond sway. A gust knocks our umbrellas together, amusing us. I point to the koi. She nods, I don't know whether in affirmation of the fish or the dragon reflection I suddenly see next.

Yellow Comfort

Chin on the sofa back, as a girl, she'd lose herself
in the spectacle of goldfinches feeding on thistle,
or by running barefoot through dandelion meadows.

She was granted a canary, to bring the outside in,
and sang with it daily, while the dwarf banana tree
yielded fruit indoors, to everyone's amazement.

Her collection of scarves in every shade of yellow,
for warmth and fashion, or fashion alone, almost
filled two wide drawers of a maple dresser.

She nearly swooned when he popped the question
with a gold engagement ring, and could not stop
saying *yes*, until he smothered her with kisses.

The kitchen wallpaper, patterned with wheat sheaves,
embraced her, like his love. Once a month she'd grate
rind for lemon poppy seed cake, his favorite.

Invariably, she would pause in the entryway
of the Chinese restaurant to study, now distractedly,
the yellow tangs in the enormous saltwater aquarium.

With her lady friends, she acted quite refined, but
was increasingly bored talking about art, and sipping
Galliano liqueur, with its top notes of vanilla and anise.

THE BURNING MOUSTACHE

Most of all she held to the sun, to deliver her
from mounting cares that were not in the plan,
which finally unraveled once she discovered, tied

in a yellow ribbon, a lock of blonde hair, so unlike
her own dull brown, lying on his desk, in plain sight.
Still, she took comfort in memories when all that was

left was the exposed incandescent bulb over her
creaky bed at the Gold Star Motel and Lounge,
and the scruffy callers with their sallow complexions.

The Leash

She came out of the animal hospital, bent,
sniffling, trying to wipe the moisture from under
her eyeglasses without taking them off.

These were the remains of her torrent
inside. She was trying to forestall the second
wave and praying for just enough composure

to make it to the car half-way down the street.
She opened the door gently and waited
for a moment before getting in, as if

she expected to be preceded. She closed it
with an equally soft touch. It took a long while
for her to start the engine, and longer

until she backed out of the diagonal space
and moved forward, leaving the quiet
side street to merge with the stream of vehicles

on the busy road to the congested highway,
where she realized she wasn't really listening
to the news, turned off the radio, and tried

to decide what to do next. Back home
in her driveway, she idled, and noticed her hand
on the steering wheel, still clutching the leash.

Final Closing Sale, Really, Final

Yes, loyal customers, this time
we really mean it. We cannot
thank you enough for your valued
patronage, 35 years of forbearance
as, each spring, we announced
our final closing sale. I assure you,
though, it was no ruse. We pride
ourselves on straight talk, fair prices,
customer satisfaction. Really,
we were ready to shut down shop
ages ago but, you know…
circumstances, family affairs,
the economy, legal wrangling,
not to mention the weather.
This is our final going out of business
sale, the one you've been waiting for.
After this weekend, we'll be history.
You're in for some incredible bargains,
folks, I assure you. We can't price
this merchandise any lower but might
be able to cut you a deal. Just don't
let my wife hear me. Step right up
while the inventory lasts because
when it's gone, it's gone, and mark
my words, you'll regret it if you miss
out. This is it, my friends. Come in.

Philip Wexler

Make me an offer. Good heavens,
is that the demolition crew
down the road? Don't be the one left
picking through the rubble on Monday
morning listening to me saying,
"I told you so." Well, I've given you
my word, and it's real, and final,
and come hell or high water,
I'll stand by it, really I will, really.

Change of Address

Don't expect to find me again.
I will be long gone, departed

from my waterlogged cardboard
shelter here by the culvert

and don't bother to follow
the informer's tip. I will already

have left the dumpster's shadow
and given up moving from one

Metro station to another,
and quit tucking myself

in between the bushes
of unsavory city parks.

That is, I'll have discovered
temporary permanence.

Call me slippery, but
I've learned my lesson well.

I will be elsewhere, still to be
determined, but be sure

Philip Wexler

I will have changed my place
of business, my domicile,

my personality, my raison d'etre.
If you need to reach me, do so

by post in care of the person
I will have become but do not

forward solicitations, bills, awards.
Let me know how you are doing.

I'll reply if you can tell me
this one time where you can be

reached. You've always been so
secretive and hard to find.

A Perfect Pair

I was on the deck, indiscriminately marveling,
on a day cruise of the Stockholm Archipelago.

An old woman in a wheelchair with a girlish
long tailed pink bow holding her platinum hair

in place rolled up beside me. Taking me
for the American I was, she asked in English

whether I had any inkling how many islands
there were. "Over 20,000," she informed me

before I could guess. In the next breath
she introduced herself as Gunilla and said

that her husband had just turned ninety.
They'd weathered other marriages, I learned,

and were newlyweds, cruising in celebration.
As I was digesting this news, a steward

materialized and unfolded two deck chairs
and a small table in front of us. On it

he centered a frosty bottle of aquavit,
the ubiquitous Scandinavian spirit,

Philip Wexler

with a Viking ship on its triangular label.
Evenly spaced around it, he placed three

diminutive etched glass tumblers and
a smorgasbord of miniature open faced

sandwiches of uncertain ingredients.
Gunilla's spry looking husband arrived.

He sat down and with an extended palm
invited me to join them. "I'm ninety,

you know, can you believe it?" I half
feigned astonishment because, of course,

I did, but not how well he carried his years.
Struggling for something to say, I settled

on *remarkable*, his cue to fill the glasses.
"You know," he said, waving a shaky finger

at the sunset, the water, and the nearest island,
"When I was young … notice I do not say

'younger,' … I would look out at the water,
an entirely different water, mind you,

and dream of Swedish girls." I laughed,
but not in disbelief, and they joined in.

THE BURNING MOUSTACHE

He stroked his bushy beard, a touch
of black remaining. "It's true, my friend,"

he added soberly. "And I of Swedish boys,"
giggled Gunilla with an impish smile.

"I'm well aware," he said. "Yes, Anders,
I know you are but I said it

for the benefit of our visitor." "So you did.
Now, how about this aquavit?" he asked,

reaching for his dose. Gunilla and I
followed his lead. We all raised our glasses

and toasted to the sunset with a hearty *skål*.
I drank up right away but Gunilla and Anders

held off, entwining their drinking arms and
adding a second, this time whispered, toast,

their eyes fixed upon each other for long
drawn out seconds that I felt might

never end but that I broke the spell
by enjoining them with a *cheers*.

They smiled broadly, and downed
their drinks, a perfect pair.

II

Winter

Rebuke
to my desire.

I've come
this far

I might as well
just quit,

let myself be
nudged to the brink,

heave
my withered

carcass over the cliff
where mammoth

shadows hover,
disputing my fate.

A hole in the ice
confounds my steps.

I sink
onto my knees.

Philip Wexler

It's not my image
down below,

it's me. I drop
my spear and freeze.

Outliers

1.

Intractable layer of snow, persisting
on the rise in the backyard's corner,
a harbor for the coldest air. Cloistered
from sun, shadowed by bamboo,
it will dissipate in its own sweet time.

2.

Brown, brittle, intransigent branch of leaves
hangs on well into spring even as clusters
of fresh green unfold on every side. Lucky
it's too high for the perfectionist gardener
with her sharp shears to reach.

3.

The only apartment with light streaming
out its windows at 3 AM, an anomaly
in the black facade of sleep. Do they
celebrate or dispute? Are they smashed
or are they out making their own rules?

4.

Two years now, they are without the cat.
The sofa has been brushed, vacuumed,

shampooed. How is it two white hairs
persist on the red satin seat cushion?
No sense picking them off.

5.

Mute for ten years, she has heard enough
of them saying, without bothering to whisper,
that she is become no more than a vegetable.
When her husband returns to reconcile,
she gives voice to ear splitting decibels.

6.

The party goes on around him. Hunched
in front of his monitor, he won't budge
from his desk. He shrugs off invitations
to dance, drink. A purple crepe streamer
lands on his keyboard. He blows it away.

Focus

Sipping tea at the sunny kitchen table,
in between flips of newspaper pages,
I look up at the African Violet
centerpiece, profusely lavender.
I push it back to make more room
for the paper where I spot, buried

on page 3 of the Metro section,
a story on last week's shooting
outside a school. At the funeral,
the mother of twin girls presses
flowers against her chest, her chin
crushing them from above. Raising

my head to view the scene outside
the window, I see a boy riding
a tricycle under the watchful eyes
of his nanny. Behind a fence, his dog
barks for freedom. I shove the paper
aside, move the African Violet closer.

November Brown

tobacco and tortoise
shell comb,
crisp Bosc pears,
russet autumn leaves,
acorns under oaks,
chocolate and almond,
a swirl of flavors,
see-through pepper
grinder, pretzels,
shoelaces, rusted keys,
cinnamon on oatmeal,
a caked paint brush,
thin and fragrant
vanilla beans,
trunks and branches,
weathered bark,
muddy streams,
dark and glistening
coffee beans,
chestnuts in a heap,
pine cone and violin,
all the seeds
under all the earth,
blotted out overnight –
December White.

Prayer for the Windlorn

God, why
did you rescind
the wind?
In stillness
I crumple.
In its rush
I heard the word,
your voice,
the world
I sought.
Won't you restore
in full this forceful
void to rescue and
revive me?
The sun,
  take that instead.
It never warmed
  my heart.
The calm
  does not calm me.
Without the wind
to push against
and fill me up and
lift me high,
I'm slack,
for it defines

Philip Wexler

my vertical
and soaring
to be yours.
Return, I pray,
my gust of life
so I may stay
your constant kite.

The Bay

Spectrum of sailboats,
    blue, white, yellow,
bob on the inlet
    close by the pier.
Superimposed on soft
    cushy mountains,
a looming red
    suspension bridge,
its roadway strung
    with pinprick lights.
Sketchy horizontal clouds
    dissipate as you watch.
Under the bridge, balanced
    on the horizon's
taut wire for a moment,
    the round sun, before
it fades to shapeless light.
    Gusts of wind
turn water's scallop
    waves to choppy
diamonds, skin of a giant
    reptile exiting hibernation.
Faint fingernail moon
    is suddenly alive.
Forever I could follow the pair
    of gulls flying
across a sky turning
    the blue-gray
of their wings.

Modigliani is Bread

Nudes steaming fresh loaves.
Bellies pliable thighs legs all
compliant resistant to part
from dough retain elastic
sponginess. Baguette arms
breadstick fingers toes
for nibbling. Brioche
breasts rise beckon for more
kneading tasting. Flat bread
backs slope down to mounds
brimfully leavened. Clefts
creases indentations form
shapes re-form resist

pressure yield spring back.
Taut stretchy bands of skin
barest hint of crust. Filmy thin
glaze of sweet cream. Awake
asleep eyes almond contoured
flavored. Inside heat swells
elongations to maximum
curves of desire. Curlicue
swirls of rising lips demand
anointing. Modigliani is bread.
Attired in nakedness
baked concoctions of women
delicious staves of life.

The Man with the Burning Moustache

gazes up the long crowded avenue
preparing for his daily walk.
His moustache has always been burning.
No one notices it anymore
but he still feels the constant heat
on his upper lip.
The man whose moustache is on fire
braces himself for his walk.
He will have to bear the neglect
of the busy people.
He is the only one
who will not hurry.
The man whose moustache is in flames
wishes he could reap the love
of the ordinary
but not at the expense
of his moustache
for without it
he would feel nothing.
The man whose moustache
blazes red and orange and shoots
sparks into the air
looks long up the bustling avenue
wishing the fire would spread.

Complexities

Of what is said
and what is not.

Of what you are
and what you say,

the part I see,
the part I don't.

Of what you're not
and cannot be.

I read imperfectly
your face.

I hear imperfectly
your words.

We cannot quit
complexities.

You are not you,
but who am I

to question who
you are or not?

THE BURNING MOUSTACHE

I cannot claim
to know or guess

who you may be.
I am not me.

Make Believe

You do it
when no one's around
and, without stirring,
you bound over light years,
and if anyone notices
and thinks you crazy,
so much the better.

Most everything
that could happen
never does.
That's what makes it
so believable,
and it's a good thing too
or else you'd go numb
from the overload.
Making believe,
you have the heavens
at your fingertips
without the risk.

Common wisdom
calls for deep roots
that do not shift,
for a firm foundation,
impermeable, intact,

as the sole way
to make sense
of this battering
life.

You are advised
that truth can't survive
without a solid center
that steadies you
and keeps you
in one piece
but what about
the hard brittle edge
of make believe that,
breaking off as you touch it,
can hardly be called
less real?

Aquatic Airs

> "Sleep in fishes, all of which lack true eyelids,
> consists of a seemingly listless state in which
> the fish maintains its balance but moves slowly."
> —*Encyclopedia Britannica*

Sleep in fishes
moves slowly as
do fishes in sleep,
no eyelids to close,
eyes like the knots
in the oak prow
of the sunken ship.
Bubbles rise up.
Fish bedding down
in the cannons,
not worried about
the galleon's fate
which has not ended,
or their fate which
has not begun.
Fish in my closed eyes
like the knots
in the oak cupboard
where the aquarium sits.
I move in my sleep
as fish do in their water.
Plural of fish is

THE BURNING MOUSTACHE

fish or fishes
depending on your mood
and these sounds
on your lips
take you to deeper seas.
Out to their fins
they sleep and make
the water sleep too.

Before Clearing Snow

Work waits for me
    out front,
to shovel walkways
    and steps,

to clear the driveway
    and car
of a deep December
    snow.

But after 5 AM tea
    and toast,
I think I'll retire
    to the patch

of beech and pine
    out back,
while the snow is powder
    and pure,

to watch the moon fade
    from sight,
and the whiteness brighten
    with dawn.

THE BURNING MOUSTACHE

My work can wait
    for me,
while I answer
    a deeper call,

for a moment to merge
    into white,
like a snowshoe hare,
    there and gone.

III

A Closer Look

It has been falling since dawn, inching
up the steps of the portico and its floor
planks in ever lighter dustings, stopping

short of the splintered gray door. Inside,
a yellow-ribboned blonde girl makes fleshy fists
to wipe the frosty pane, presses her nose

against the glass, looks out. Papa lumbers
up from the basement, sled in tow. She has
been begging all morning, afraid the snow

wouldn't last, but he had wood to chop.
Now she's petulant, won't look back
at him. She'd rather penetrate herself

the white unflinching woods where Mamma
went, but Papa pulls her ribbons, tickles
her partway out of her moodiness.

Like an ox, he hauls her up the hill.
Several times they slide down together.
They trudge back in laughter, she in spite

of herself, content just then with the portions
that serve for wholes. Papa leans the sled
against the portico, and heads back to the wood

pile. She hurries up the steps, grips
the door knob, and can almost see Mamma
in the impression her face left on the glass.

Museum Going

The girl studying the painting of a black stallion
galloping out the gate in front of a white church
is not in the museum anymore. She is at rest

in a field, bareback on the stallion, as it grazes
on violets. The steeple is barely visible. She is
in the church looking out the window at the shut

gate and beyond at the girl in the field at peace
on the stallion. She is praying for the gate to reopen.
The girl is on a cloud shaped like a horse, air thin.

Giddy, faint, by heart she paints her desire, tosses
the brush in the lake, colors it red. She comes to
rest where she started, goes back for more.

Snow on Fifth Avenue

I was in the car
with my parents.
I was in the back, alone,
hugging a portable radio,
the birthday gift
they handed me in the car.
They were not arguing.
It was a late November
heavy snow. Now and then
I'd turn my head to look
out the rear window
to see where I had been.
I clutched the radio tightly
as if afraid to let go
of my parents. Fully
extended, the antenna
almost touched the roof.
Every so often, my mother
would stretch back to pat
my thigh affectionately
and my father would ask
"So, how's it going, champ?"
"Great!" I'd invariably say.
The radio was silent.
We were on our way
to buy batteries. Snow

swept across department
store window displays
set up for the holidays.
My father drove slowly,
his black hair glistening
from pomade.
My mother's long red hair
blanketed the back
of her seat. They spoke
calmly, sometimes touching
hands. She turned to him
often, a whisper here
and there, and I was sure
I even heard a few chuckles.
I congratulated myself
on knowing all of this
could be possible.
The green vinyl upholstery
felt luxurious to my touch,
saturated as I was with bliss.
I loved turning
the radio dial and
seeing the red line sweep
across station numbers.
The black plastic was
shiny and clean and
smelled fresh.
I crinkled a piece of
the red wrapping paper
up against my ear

Philip Wexler

for no reason other
than to hear the sound.
Lots of people were
on the sidewalks
but it sounded as quiet
and peaceful outside as in.
It went on snowing
for however long
Fifth Avenue stretched,
for however long we drove
and honestly, batteries
or no, it didn't matter
for I was so happy
with the two of them
in harmony,

did not once that day
feel like crying."

at least for a time,
that not even once
that day did I feel
like crying.

Under a Flowering Pear Tree at a Stubborn Red Light

Like tiny fists, windblown
petals harmlessly pummel
the car windows and hood

as the light refuses
to budge at this crossing,
empty but for us.

My toddler daughter
is upset with me
for taking her on this trip.

I scoop her up from the back,
hold her at arm's length,
let her punch the air.

My laughter, I'm sure,
only upsets her more
but it's just too funny.

I bring her closer
so she can pound
away at me in earnest,

but she's already vented
her anger and can't keep up
the fight or tears for long.

Philip Wexler

She goes limp, asleep
in my arms. I return her
gently to the rear carrier

where she wakes up at once,
leans forward, points
in wonder, just noticing

the swirling white petals.
"Snow," she says.
"Flowers," I correct her.

She starts to cry again.
"Alright, snow," I say.
She leans back, satisfied,

into her dreams. The light
turns green and we go wherever
it was we were headed.

What the Zoo Holds

White Bengal tiger
in his cage stalks

gazelle from a past
life. I live

in fear of something
inside myself.

A boy runs
into me, spilling

his popcorn, pointing
accusingly. His mother

tugs him away, shoots
me a deadly parting

glance. The tiger
yawns in boredom.

I scoop up popcorn,
toss it through the bars.

If I had a rifle, I might
taunt him better.

He reads my motives
and growls.

grandmother in sweater

picking cucumbers from baskets
in the market on Tuesday morning,
in sweater contradicting the summer,
lowering her glasses, peering closely
at the size and shape and surface,
checking for protuberances that belong
and those that trespass according to her
particular standards of perfection,
checking the green of the green, and the yellow
of the yellow, holding each at arm's length
up to the sky, as if posing them for a painting,
squeezing without embarrassment, to test
firmness, temporarily setting aside all other
contemplation, even of grandchildren,
making a nice selection, taking a crunchy
bite from one or another she has picked
and telling the farmer weighing her crop
to charge her for an extra ounce or two,
on that account, which he never does.

Fishing by Mistake

You had other things on the agenda
      for that sweltering Sunday -
wax the car, pull up weeds, patch
      the shaky flagstone steps.

You hastily scribbled a list
      on the back
of a stray grocery receipt, in tiny,
      insincere script and put it

on the passenger seat next to you.
      But at the second light,
instead of turning right
      to the hardware store

for the paste wax, you veered
      left. A scrap
of paper flew out
      the window, and soon

you discovered a place
      from long ago - water,
a lichen covered boulder
      and a dragonfly sewing

in the air, its narrow
      shadow jiggling

Philip Wexler

across your rod, flexed
      with the pull of a bite.

It wasn't how you planned it
      but you didn't regret being
naked in the sunlight,
      fishing by mistake.

The Calling

In my assigned seat at the back
of the Brooklyn classroom,
my first objective was to survive
roll call. Then, by dodging
and crouching, my hope
was to make myself invisible
enough not to be called on,
to be left alone at least
for a brief stretch of morning.

Once the lesson started,
Mrs. Valentine's voice blended
with the traffic noise, creating
a white noise backdrop
to my musings. My classmates
raised hands left and right,
trying to outdo each other
to impress her, gaining me
the time I needed to migrate

to my private zone. This day
it was in the direction of Alice
Flores who sat in front of me.
Without her knowledge, I lifted
her pony tail bound
in a thin white band onto my desk
and held on to it gently.

Philip Wexler

In an instant I was in Veracruz,
an Aztec scout, checking
the advance of Cortés and his troops.
Alice was at my side, already
a fully developed woman
in a feathered cloak trimmed
with rabbit fur. Our expedition
was a hodgepodge of old history
lessons I had only half paid
attention to and couldn't fit together.

Outside our camp, the sound
of the sea and the clattering of warriors
come from a distant shore,
salivating at the prospect of conquest.
I replayed in my mind the voices
of the elders relaying messages
from the spirit world, outlining
my path and fate. I was fortified
by Alice's pledge, the treasure
that would be ours,
and the coronation to come.
I saddled and mounted
my white horse, still a novelty
for our tribe, and bent down
so Alice could bid me farewell
with a kiss. My compatriots
cheered and then – another voice,
Mrs. Valentine's, calling my name,
once, twice, followed
by the blast of a car horn.

THE BURNING MOUSTACHE

I let go of Alice's hair.
She and the rest of the class turned
en masse to face me. I was startled,
unsure whether I was leaving
or entering a daydream. I wanted
to escape but my horse was gone.
Mrs. Valentine asked me where
exactly I thought I was.
There was no use explaining
when I could see that not even Alice
with her sympathetic but shallow
eyes realized we were
in ancient Mexico together,
steps away from salvaging
our race and fulfilling our destiny.

The Kitten

The snow let up.
My mother brushed
the accumulation

from my collar
as we walked.
A kitten shivered

at the base of a drift.
Black, save for a blotch
of pink around the nose.

I lifted it up
to bring home.
No resistance on its part

but my mother said, "No."
I plunged my bottom
into the snow, holding

tight. My mother said,
"It's cold." She grabbed
my hand, pulled.

The kitten escaped
behind some trash
cans. It started snowing

again. I lost sight.
I was too helpless
to do anything

but let myself be led.
The apartment was warm.
I wanted to run away.

Grandmother with Tubes

Going in, coming out.
Pumping into her - drugs
and semblances of food, air.

Extracting - waste
that would otherwise
dribble immodestly.

Her body, recently passable,
at least workable,
finally sunk down

to the level of her mind,
hazy, clouded, barely
conscious for three years,

though hints were there
much earlier. Angled
on a lofty throne-like bed,

grandmother is stuck
with tubes, her hands
restrained so she can't pull

them out. Here we pace
along three sides
of her perimeter

THE BURNING MOUSTACHE

as she prepares
for an even longer term
position. Here we are

being asked to make
decisions, with no one
to advise what's right.

There she ebbs, mute,
helplessly going
down the tubes.

We look. We look
away, as helpless,
as mute.

Stray Bullet

Her brother, crying, told Momma it was a rock
came in through the open window hit his sister
hard on the forehead while they were playing
checkers and that's why she fell. After all,
it wasn't unusual for rocks to fly through.
But it was a bullet made the stain,
hard to see, in the dark red carpet,
and Momma knew the minute she came in,
but it took the hospital hours to tell her
that her baby girl would live, a miracle.
On the street, nobody saw a thing,
or so they say. That's the way it is
in this neighborhood – bullets, on target
or off; somebody getting insulted or excited,
or shortchanged; an argument over a girl
or a pair of shoes; the wrong look,
the wrong word, and nobody thinking
about what the weary looking lady
with the shopping cart trudging
to her building who can't wait
to be in sight of her two kids will be in for
in a few minutes. No, just everybody wanting
to be in on something right here, right now,
wanting more of what they can grab.
Meanwhile the brother and sister, somehow
immune, somehow shielded, but who knows

for how long, play checkers in the kitchen,
next to the window, to taste the sun, feel
the breeze and mistake what they are
breathing in for fresh air.
They turn up the volume on the ancient
tabletop radio, to block out the drugged up
cursing outside, but not too loud,
so they can hear Momma's footsteps
and the syncopated clacking
of the shopping cart wheels on the stairs.
They anticipate the smells of her cooking,
and filling their bellies with her
delicious food, not their hearts with her
dependable love, which they'll get anyway.
And so, it happens that a boy can mistake
a bullet for a rock, or a girl can get laid out
flat, and count herself lucky if she comes out
of it, and if she's got a Momma
that even gives a damn that she does.

Swamp Monster

I'm ten years old, watching a horror movie
in my friend, Joey's, basement, a musty

place, rain pelting the lone window
behind his old man, Lenny, fat, asleep,

hopelessly sunk in a plush green chair,
magazine on his lap, eyeglasses perched

like a confused bird, on the tip
of his bulbous nose. During commercials,

I stare at Lenny's head as it ratchets down bit
by bit. The moment chin grazes collar,

it jerks back up, and the sequence repeats,
immune to the rattling thunder outside.

Joey ignores him, and asks me what
I'm looking at. I say I'm checking out

the rain. It's slowing down. The movie
ends with a shot of the swamp monster

herded by cawing black birds back
to his home and his stepwise sinking

into the gurgling muck. We take it
as one big joke. Outside, the rain lets up.

We hop on our bikes for a ride to the lake,
leaving the old man to his murky dreams.

Tousle-Haired Kid

He was running into the big box store
as I lumbered out. His hair, dirty

blonde, was wind tunneled out
of shape, but that wasn't the point.

His yellow shirt, unbuttoned,
untucked, waved like a flag.

It wasn't that either, but these props
stick with me just as much. What

it was – his eyes, our eyes converging
for a second, my seeing what he saw

in me – himself, fast forwarded
to my gray state, a flash

of recognition, even a shudder
at his future, before he hurried on

into the store, catching up, now
I realized, with friends already there,

to continue being an unreflective
kid, as well he should. I trudged

THE BURNING MOUSTACHE

to my final destination, closer
but no less predictable than his.

I hope, someday, when troubles drag
him down, he will remember me.

The Little Princess was Running

You wouldn't expect it,
with her gown and crown
and jeweled shoes,

but she was a child,
running with a boy
and a yellow ball.

"And what will you be?"
she asked him.
"Surely not a prince?"

"Prince? No," he laughed.
"A bull, I might
become a bull."

"Right now, you mean,
or when you're older?
Come, tell."

"When you go away."
He spun the ball
on one finger. It dropped.

"And what about me?
Will I be
a princess always?"

THE BURNING MOUSTACHE

"Always."
She dribbled the ball
and he stole it back.

"And what else?"
"You'll stop running,"
said the boy.

"Will there be anything
wrong with that?"
she inquired.

"You'll still want to,"
he said, and bounced
the yellow ball off

his head, straight
into the hoop she made
with her arms.

IV

The Ball Rolling

She came into your office as she'd done
many times, to tell you exactly what
she needed, and you spelled it out
precisely, omitting no detail, adding
nothing extra. Standing, she looked down
at her shoes, and you, from your chair,
out the window, and then she was gone,
mission, on the surface, accomplished
to the both of your everlasting satisfactions.

A few hours later you thought of a reason
to go to her office, something optional
you'd meant to note, a "by the way."
Behind her desk, she listened, fidgeting
with a set of keys. You leaned
against a bookcase for support. She agreed
with everything you said, and you wanted
to say more but couldn't, and she seemed
to want to further your cause, if only

you could get the ball rolling.

Bounty

The swaying of your hips
on the old fruit tree's limb.
Reaching for the apples

of your eyes, you are
the apple of mine. I am off-
balanced by the beauty,

not the risk. I am hoping
you fall – backwards
into my arms. You rock

from side to side
but the tree won't part
with any part of you

as you toss Golden
Delicious, one after another,
onto the feather blanket

spread underneath.
One gets away, rolls
on the ground to me.

I bite, chew, slowly, watch
you keep plucking, tossing,
with both hands, bounty.

THE BURNING MOUSTACHE

You pivot from the waist, pitch
your shoulders, simmer
me like apples into sauce.

Archaeology

Afterwards, she sits up,
draws the kimono
around her body

and turns away from me.
Jet black tresses pause
on ivory silk.

She lifts her hair
above her head. I pull
the garment down again.

Her back undraped –
red and white peonies
on Japanese porcelain.

Midnight Watch

We exhausted speech, but didn't have enough.
I took her hand. To our surprise, our watches
matched, each the low-end model of a high end
brand, French, advertised in the best magazines.
Black leather bands, ivory faces, hers half the size
of mine. Her hands and numerals silvery,
mine black. Her time was right, she said,
but I was running fast. The watches were the first
things to unclasp. We lay them side by side
on the bed stand where, long into the night,
at intervals, we heard conjoined, insistent ticking.

The Pears

We pick them from our tree, roll
them wobbly in a brown and green
blur down the slope to the crates
by the van, to pack and haul them
off to give as gifts to friends.
What's left belongs to us.

In three days when they're ripe,
we take a bunch back to the tree
to picnic on with wine and cheese.
The juice runs down our chins,
while napkins blow away,
and we make sloppy love.

Silk

In your eyes,
reflections of the lake,

turquoise, tranquil,
while you paint on silk.

Bubbles surface
and my hand extends

but you are focused,
tap aside my approach.

I am patient.
We are speechless

at the shore. A boat
sets anchor and bobs.

Silk throw protects
your knees from the sun.

Your hand probes
for the finest brush.

The sun is briefly
shielded by clouds.

Philip Wexler

This, the barest thread
of an excuse, is enough

to make silk yield.
You set aside the brush,

bare your knees, giving
me the time I need

before you pick up
where you left off.

Finishing touches
make all the difference.

Snow

Falls over us
on the footbridge,
swirls
in the mountains.
The lake
begins to freeze.
Our feet
are cold.
We leave tracks
on the snow.
Your cheeks
are roses.
We blow smoke
at each other.
On the other side
of the lake,
our hut.
We will thaw
by burning logs,
drink
green tea,
and watch the footprints
we left
on the bridge
filling up
with snow.

star magnolia

at dawn of spring,
a burst of white
careless petals,
half-drooping,
sticking up
this way, down
that, unposed,
beautiful, half
naked woman
waking up
disheveled
to her own
eyes,
fully realized
and not to be
improved upon
to his.

Gelato

He cradles a single
white paper cup.

Half mango – her portion,
half lemon – his.

White plastic spoons,
scoops tiny

as fingernails.
Delicately, they lap

their respective flavors,
she more slowly. One

swallow, then another,
making a game

of respecting the border.
Finishing the lemon,

he encroaches
on her mango,

smacks his lips
at the ripe taste.

Philip Wexler

Her face radiates
mock amazement.

The spoon slips
from her hand.

She loops her arm
through his.

He finishes
everything left.

Combing

Hooked arm in arm, her boyfriend
whisked her into the elevated line car.

They faced forward in a double seat.
A cold wind had wreaked havoc

with her hair. Incessantly, she fussed
with it. No brush, comb, mirror – none

needed. She didn't even consult
her reflection in the window. All

instinct. She knew by feel how to restore
the part, comb stray strands, set the right

bunches behind her ears, making sure
nothing stuck up that shouldn't,

and adjusted her barrette so it held
down the locks it was meant to –

all accomplished with fingers and palms,
while debating with her boyfriend

about the movie they had seen.
He hated it. She loved it. But

Philip Wexler

they agreed they were very much like
the main characters. He paid no mind

to the magic she was working. Getting
her hair settled, she signaled receptiveness

to a kiss, and he complied, long
and deep and unrestrained. She lay

her head on his shoulder. Her barrette
unclasped, undoing her handiwork,

sending her hair flying in newfound
disarray, fraying from the static of his

woolen topcoat. Haphazardly, he ran
his fingers through it unchallenged.

Already There

You are running
    late again.

I've been all ready
    for hours.

Your excuses
    are too much to bear.

I grab the map,
    and rush away

like angry steam.
    I'm halfway down

the empty street
    when you catch up.

You cup my chin,
    like a chalice,

in your palm,
    and with your pleading

eyes, look for a drop
    of yourself in mine,

and pry loose
    the fingers

of my fist. The map
    slips out.

Can't I see,
    you implore,

there's nowhere
    else to go.

We are
    already there.

So, we continue,
    hand in hand.

Cashmere

You embroider me
a scarf, camouflaging

our intertwined names
in elaborate Celtic knots

so I'll slow down,
think of you. Keeping

warm is not the point.
You double stitch

the edges so I won't
fray. I want you

to trust in my velocity
and oscillations.

You are determined
to rein me in though

I'll have none of it. Here -
at least let's sip some

brandy. I never was
a scarf person,

Philip Wexler

too confining. Same
with ties. Can't abide

them. I'm surprised
you didn't guess.

I don't mean to be
ungrateful for the gift.

Wool, even cashmere
itches me but I don't

fault you for trying
all you know.

I'll display the scarf
like a work of art

on my front closet door
if that will take away

the sting. Just let's not
get tied up in knots.

Broken Yellow

Oufitted with jackhammers,
I drill relentlessly
into a tropical sun
to escape her petitions.
Sparks fly
through hot caverns.

Broken yellow
left me
her calling card.
I wasn't home.
Out struggling
with buried communication
lines, repairing
splicing,
altering, frayed,
fossilized conversations.

For the last few miles
I toss aside
my power tools,
and take up a spade,
a spoon,
my fingers.
I dig.
I dial.

Philip Wexler

Getting through
to Central
I am told how
they spied her
in brief
diaphanous silks,
dressed to kill,
hovering over
my vacated chambers.

That day outside
My shuttered door,
that blistering day,
she was ablaze
but I was digging
a different sun.

Inside the Picket Fence

I am full from dinner
but the chicken left
such a mess.

I can't bear this nonsense
but its freezing outside.

I wish the table was clean
but I won't lift a finger.

I wish it would never snow
or the snow would continue
indefinitely until I see
nothing but white.
It's sad to live with slush.

Out of the white snow I wish
for a Chinese woman
with a rice paper umbrella.

She would be happy
encountering no one
but not disappointed
to see me.

Autumn Knowledge

Under cloud cover one would
not look twice at the lawn
but when the sun comes out
the fading grass is like
a well-worn Persian rug
covered with golden Ginkgo leaves
and dried out chrysanthemums.
The leaves still falling could be
feathers of golden owls
startled out of sleep.

The man with the rake
notices none of it.
On his mind is a woman
who took it upon herself
to instruct him in too much.
He makes little piles of gold
and is glad he knows enough.

Eating Kisses

It was finally arranged.
She'd meet me at the fountain

of Bacchus in front of the wine
bar named in his honor. I sat

on a redwood bench,
a deluxe box of chocolate

kisses, wrapped in glittery purple
foil, on my lap. People sipped

wine at slotted redwood tables
under a white canvas awning.

After waiting twenty minutes,
I ordered a glass of burgundy

and resolved to give it twenty more.
When the time came, I paid,

and stepped up to the stone circle
surrounding the water. I stared

at the reflection of Bacchus'
bronze face, and my own,

Philip Wexler

before seeing hers. But
when I turned, I realized it was

the waving yellow switchgrass
colluding with her absence.

A pair of couples at one of the tables
gratefully accepted the chocolates.

I headed off, but not before eating,
at their urging, a few kisses myself.

Their Morning in Flannels

He sits at the table screaming.
She stands at the stove scrambling.

He asks for answers, reasons.
she dices, sprinkles spices.

He is spitting mad, glares.
She fries and trembles, cries.

He accuses, fumes, threatens.
She denies, pleads, arranges plates.

She takes the offensive, ridiculing,
pressing for confessions, motives.

He defends, rebuts, deflects.
She throws down the silverware,

tells him to get his own damn juice.
His neck tightens, turns red.

She brings the omelet to the table and sits.
"It needs more salt, Cynthia, as usual."

"Oh, Jim, let's put it aside." She touches
his shoulder. Tentatively, they kiss.

Philip Wexler

A solitary woman pauses outside
the window, latches on to the momentary

kiss, thinks how lucky they are,
how she longs for such a life.

She resumes walking. In the kitchen,
they wave knives at each other.

Out Back

We went to the backyard of the empty house
in the evenings, after work, after we bought it,
but before we moved in or even had the keys.
We went to listen to the cricket sounds of August
and the leaves of the bamboo brushing against
each other in the warm wind, honeysuckle dense
and fragrant, nestling around us on three sides,
and count the few stars through suburban haze.
We strained to hear the muffled traffic, feared
oh, no, it's too close to the highway, and then, no,
it's not that bad, really. We wondered, each of us
separately, we divulged later, what it would be
like to live under one roof. It seemed so wondrous
and strange. It doesn't anymore. We don't anymore.

The Continuity of Disentanglement

Strands of her hair work their way up
    out of the upholstery.
I notified the post office twice
    but they still deliver her mail.
In a compartment of her shoe organizer,
    another of the empty pickle jars
she obsessively stockpiled
    throughout the apartment.
I can't get out of the habit of tanking up
    at the rock-bottom priced
gas station we discovered together –
    no sense passing up a bargain
just to flush her from my mind.
    The dry cleaners ask after her,
the arts and crafts store, the diner.
    Friends I rarely hear from
start calling and want to know
    everything. A bottle
of cabernet from the casualty
    of her most recent disentanglement
left at my door with a note –
    "Don't let it get to you,
man; she's poison."
    My helplessness at her scent,
lingering or imagined, intruding
    on my senses and good sense.

THE BURNING MOUSTACHE

Her tile painting of a blue jay,
    for my birthday, inscribed
in the corner with her initials and a heart.
    The boxy green subcompact
I'm left with, the one I swore
    I'd never drive until, that is,
the SUV took flight with her.
    Out of boredom, my flipping
the pages of her dessert cookbook
    to find her stirring
the batter of a lemon poppy seed cake,
    the photo nestling
against its recipe. Dreams?
    Too many. Too vivid. Too much.
As for the lamp with the low wattage
    bulb on her side of the bed,
I have little occasion to turn it on anymore.
    It almost blinds me when I do.

Chives

Magically, it seemed,
    you appeared
    in the yard
offering me
    the rusty trowel
    you had taken
by mistake
    when you left.
    My grip
on the shiny new one
    loosened
    and I let it fall
in the leaf litter.
    I was primed
    to plunge
it into the soil
    to transplant
    the chives
you had started from seed.
    As I let you slide
    the weathered wooden
handle of the old tool
    into my hand,
    our fingers touched
and I started.
    We looked
    at each other
and then away.
    You sank

        into the pink
webbed lawn chair,
        you had bought
        over my objections,
and settled snugly
        into the impression
        it still carried
of your body.
        With the old trowel
        I dug up
the chives
        and split
        the clump in two.
I extended a bunch
        to you, letting
        it hover
close to your chest.
        You gently pressed
        my hand and the chives
down to your lap.
        As my fingers loosened,
        the cluster rolled
to the ground
        next to its companion.
        I let my hand, palm up
rest on your knee.
        Our eyes met again
        and I wondered whether
you, too, wanted to ask
        if we couldn't
        keep it together.

Perfectly Blind

Her pledges, at the outset, sincere, genuine
and most of all, honored. Thus, you took refuge
for a spell in the mirage of perfection. Inevitably,

the sheen began to tarnish. She was too quick
to give assurances. Her smiles were forced,
her air distracted, her look distant, lackluster.

She followed through without enthusiasm
or partway, or late, reminders notwithstanding,
or not at all. She didn't care. She'd shrug

it off. This falling away which in the day
would have struck you as impossible is, plain
and simple, the destiny you share and bear.

Looking back, you see the signs you missed.
The fault had been there all along, in wait
until the time it would reveal itself, deep, wide,

roaring, a chasm as she and your faith in her fall
out from under you. As you drop you ask yourself
how you could have been so blind for so long.

The Connection

She had just begun a letter to me
when I called, how prescient.

I asked what it was about and she said
she couldn't hear me, a poor connection,

but I'd read it soon enough. She didn't ask
me why I called, just wished I'd let her go

so she could finish the letter. She shouted
"Goodbye" as if I couldn't hear her,

but she was crystal clear. She wouldn't hang
up, though, until I said it too, but I wanted

to talk about our drifting apart. She said
she didn't know what I was saying,

and anyway, wanted to get back to the letter
and that I was tying up her line.

She asked if I had said goodbye yet, uncertain
because of the connection. "No," I shouted.

"Fine," she screamed, and told me
she'd be wrapping the phone

Philip Wexler

in a dish towel and laying it down.
I kept talking, no word of reply from her.

After a few minutes she was back, upset
that my muffled voice was seeping

through the towel and keeping her
from finishing even the first line of the letter

about how maybe we were just too much
together to begin with. Was I ready to say

goodbye yet she wanted to know. "No,"
I shouted. "Fine," she screamed again.

I told her not to stand on ceremony
and hang up already if that's what she wanted.

When suddenly she did, I fell silent, resigned
to wait for her letter. A moment later

when my phone rang, it was her,
saying we must have been disconnected.

Turn Out the Light

The light at the end
of the canal
shines softly at night
while the water glistens.

What it means
is hidden in
street lamps
in a restless city
far from the canal
and sleep.

You cup
some water
in your hands
and carry the reflection
away from all
beginnings.

The canal remains
part water
part darkness.

In a brilliant city
a neon light
malfunctions.

Disengagement
is on your mind
and the water
in the canal
is dark
as a pillow.

You want
to sleep
because her hair
is too blonde
on the pillow.

Turn out the light
because the city
is too bright
to sleep with you.
And then turn
to the night again.

About the Author

Phil Wexler has been writing poetry his entire adult life. Originally from New York City, he spent his formative years in Brooklyn before moving, as a young man, to Bethesda, Maryland, a suburb of Washington, DC.

Phil has some 170 literary magazine publications to his credit. Although his focus has always been poetry, including prose poetry, he has dipped into the waters of fiction with several short stories. His collection of prose poems, The Sad Parade, was published by Adelaide Books in 2019. He has organized and emceed a number of spoken word reading series over the years in the DC area. Most recently, he oversees the monthly Words out Loud at Glen Echo Park in Maryland, which includes featured readers, an open mic, and a literary trivia quiz. While in New York, his many literary haunts included the Strand Bookstore and the Unterberg Poetry Center of the 92nd Street Y and, if he just wanted a drink, there was always McSorley's Old Ale House and The White Horse Tavern. He is a long-time member of The Writer's Center in Bethesda and tries to take advantage of the DC area's vibrant literary scene there and elsewhere, such as the Politics and Prose bookstore.

Phil has edited and authored numerous book and journal technical publications in the fields of toxicology informatics and toxicology history. These include serving as Editor-in-Chief of The Encyclopedia of Toxicology, 4th edition (in progress) and Information Resources in Toxicology, 5th edition (2020), as well as series editor for a monographic series, History of Toxicology and Environmental Health, all published by Elsevier. He is also editor of Chemicals, Environment Health: A Global Management Perspective (2011. CRC Press) and co-editor-in-chief of the journal, Global Security: Health, Science and Policy (Taylor and Francis). He is a member of the US Society of Toxicology (SOT) and a recipient of its Public Communications Award (2010), and a Trustee with the Toxicology Education Foundation (TEF). Phil has taught, given technical presentations, and organized public outreach events related to toxicology, internationally. After a long career of government service as a Technical Information Specialist, he retired from the Toxicology and Environmental Health Information Program of the National Library of Medicine, an arm of the National Institutes of Health, in 2018.

In addition to writing, Phil is also passionate about the arts in general and his work as a non-commercial mosaic artist. He is an avid museum- and theater-goer, and a fan of opera and Broadway musicals. Over the years, he has also been intermittently immersed in pursuits as varied as bicycle touring, hiking, fencing, indoor and outdoor gardening, and being overly attentive to he and his wife's dog, Gigi. He tries to keep up with the increasingly crazy global and domestic news and is very concerned about the state of our environment. He is married to Nancy and has one son, Jake.

www.ingramcontent.com/pod-product-compliance
Lightning Source LLC
Chambersburg PA
CBHW032229080426
42735CB00008B/777